dabble lab

10-MINUTE NO-SEW PROJECTS

BY ELSIE OLSON

CAPSTONE PRESS
a capstone imprint

Dabble Lab is published by Capstone Press, a Capstone imprint.
1710 Roe Crest Drive, North Mankato, Minnesota 56003
capstonepub.com

Library of Congress Cataloging-in-Publication Data
Names: Olson, Elsie, 1986- author.
Title: 10-minute no-sew projects / by Elsie Olson.
Description: North Mankato, Minnesota : Capstone Press, an imprint of
Capstone, [2022] | Series: 10-minute makers | Includes bibliographical
references. | Audience: Ages 8-11 | Audience: Grades 4-6 | Summary:
"Looking for quick and easy no-sew projects for your makerspace? Look
no further! From stuffed animals and superhero masks to flowers and
finger puppets, these amazing 10-minute fabric projects will have kids
making in no time!"– Provided by publisher.
Identifiers: LCCN 2021029672 (print) | LCCN 2021029673 (ebook) |
ISBN 9781663959034 (hardcover) | ISBN 9781666322149 (pdf) |
ISBN 9781666322163 (kindle edition)
Subjects: LCSH: Textile crafts–Juvenile literature. | Handicraft for
children–Juvenile literature.
Classification: LCC TT699 .O47 2022 (print) | LCC TT699 (ebook) |
DDC 745.5083–dc23
LC record available at https://lccn.loc.gov/2021029672
LC ebook record available at https://lccn.loc.gov/2021029673

Image Credits
Project photos: Mighty Media, Inc.
Shutterstock Images, p. 24 (hook)

Design Elements
Shutterstock Images

Editorial Credits
Editor: Liz Salzmann
Production Specialist: Aruna Rangarajan

All internet sites appearing in back matter were available and accurate when
this book was sent to press.

Printed and bound in the USA. PO4608

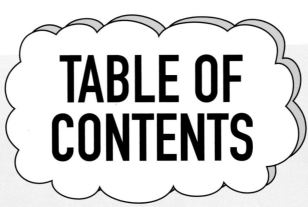

TABLE OF CONTENTS

GOT 10 MINUTES?

Gather some fabric, fire up your hot glue gun, and get ready to craft. In minutes, you can create a truly terrific tapestry, a fabulous flannel bouquet, and more. The best part? These quick and easy projects will leave you with loads of time to clean up when you're finished!

General Supplies and Tools

buttons

cardboard

fabric scraps
(felt, flannel,
old clothes)

felt

fiberfill stuffing

hot glue gun

markers

old socks

puffy paint

rubber bands

ruler or measuring
tape

scissors

string

Tips

- Before starting a project, read the instructions. Then gather the supplies and tools you'll need.

- You can cut apart old clothes to make fabric scraps. Just be sure to ask an adult for permission before destroying anything!

- Fabric scissors cut fabric more easily than regular scissors. If you have fabric scissors, don't use them to cut anything but fabric! This will keep them nice and sharp.

- Ask an adult to help you with sharp or hot tools.

- Change things up! Don't be afraid to make these projects your own.

SNUGGLY SOCK OWL

Upcycle an old sock into a cuddly woodland buddy.
You could display it in your room or give it as a gift.

What You Need:

- scissors (fabric)
- old sock
- ruler or measuring tape
- mini rubber bands
- fiberfill stuffing
- hot glue gun
- buttons

What You Do:

1 Cut the toe off the sock to make a tube. Cut a vertical slit about ½ inch (1.3 centimeters) long through both layers on each end of the tube.

2 Make ears by twisting a mini rubber band around the fabric on either side of the slit on one tube end. Stuff fiberfill through the open end to fill the sock.

3 Twist mini rubber bands around the fabric on each side of the open end's slit to make legs. Twist a rubber band around the middle of the sock to make a head.

4 Cut up and glue on pieces of the toe to make wings and a beak. Glue on button eyes.

TIP Don't have fiberfill stuffing? Use cotton balls, newspaper, or fabric scraps left over from other projects to stuff your fluffy pal.

FANTASTIC FLAG BANNER

Put your own stamp on this festive banner. It's perfect for a special occasion or to celebrate every day!

What You Need:

scissors (both craft & fabric)

cardboard

marker

fabric

paint & foam brush

rubber stamp

string

What You Do:

1 Cut a triangle out of cardboard. This will be a template.

2 Use a marker to trace the template eight to ten times on the back of your fabric. Cut each triangle out to make flags.

3 Fold one edge of each flag. Cut a slit in each corner. This makes two holes in each flag. Unfold the flags.

4 Coat the stamp with paint. Press it onto the flags. Let the paint dry.

5 Cut a length of string about 5 feet (1.5 meters) long. Thread it through the holes to complete your banner!

TIP Add more color to your banner by including some flags cut out of different fabrics. Just follow steps 2 and 3 to make the extra flags.

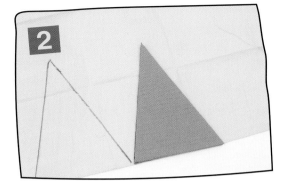

SQUISHY DONUT

This supersoft stocking donut might not taste sweet, but it makes a darling decoration!

10

What You Need:

old pair of tights or stockings
scissors (fabric)
puffy fabric paint
beads & clear glue (optional)

What You Do:

1 If you're using tights, cut the legs off to make stockings. Cut the toes off each stocking to make two long tubes of fabric.

2 Starting at one end, roll the tube inside out into a ring shape.

3 Push the second tube of fabric through the ring's hole. Wrap the end of the tube around the ring.

4 Roll the tube around the ring to thicken the ring into a donut shape.

5 Frost your donut with puffy paint. If you want, glue on beads to add some sprinkles.

FLANNEL FLOWERS

Snip and fold an old flannel shirt into a sweet flannel flower.
If you have extra time, make several and create a bouquet!

What You Need:

marker

drinking glass

old flannel shirt or fabric

felt

scissors (fabric)

hot glue gun

button

chenille stem

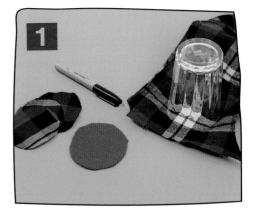

What You Do:

1 Trace the drinking glass 12 times on the flannel and 1 time on the felt. Cut out each circle.

2 Stack three flannel circles together. Fold the stack once and then again to make a triangle.

3 Clip the pointed tip off the triangle. Glue that same end of the triangle to the center of the felt.

4 Repeat steps 2 and 3 with the remaining flannel circles. Glue a button in the middle of the flower.

5 Glue a chenille stem to the back of the flower to make a stem.

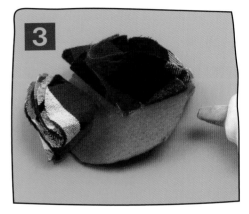

TIP Speed up your cutting by stacking or folding your flannel or fabric. This will allow you to cut out multiple circles at once!

13

COZY WATER BOTTLE HOLDER

Make a soft water bottle cover out of a
bubble envelope and a sock!

What You Need:

bubble mailing envelope

scissors

duct tape

water bottle

old sock

string, buttons & hot glue gun (optional)

What You Do:

1 Cut the envelope so it fits around the bottle and is about three-fourths of the bottle's height. Wrap the envelope around the bottle. Tape the seam.

2 Remove the water bottle. Push the envelope tube into the sock. Fold the sock over the end of the tube.

3 Push the bottle back into the tube.

4 If you want to, glue on a bow, buttons, or other decorations.

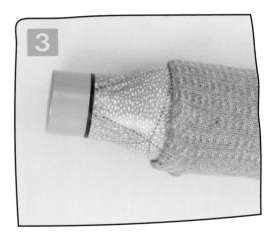

MAGNIFICENT MASK

Become your own hero and design a mask to match!
What's your name? What are your powers?
Let your super-identity inspire the look.

What You Need:

paper

marker

scissors

felt

hot glue gun

gems or other decorative materials

elastic cord

ruler or measuring tape

What You Do:

1 Draw your mask on paper. Cut it out. Hold it over your face to make sure the eyeholes are in the right place! This will be your template.

2 Trace the template on felt. Cut out the shape and the eyeholes.

3 Decorate your mask! Glue on felt shapes, gems, or other materials.

4 Cut a small hole on each side of the mask. Be careful not to cut through the edge of the felt.

5 Cut a length of elastic cord 12 inches (30.5 cm) long. Tie one end through each of the holes you made in step 4.

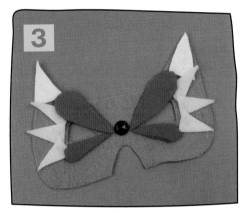

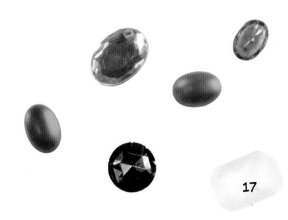

BANDANNA BRACELET

An old shower curtain ring and a bandanna can become a stylish bracelet. Make one for yourself and one for a friend!

What You Need:

old bandanna or fabric

scissors (fabric)

ruler or measuring tape

round shower curtain ring

clear glue, gems, sequins & other decorations (optional)

What You Do:

1 Cut a strip of bandanna that is about 2 inches (5 cm) wide.

2 Starting in middle of the strip, wrap the fabric around the ring until the entire ring is covered.

3 Tie the ends of the strip. You can either leave the ends intact as decoration or trim them off.

4 If you want, glue on gems, sequins, or other decorations.

TIP If shower curtain rings are too small, you can also use embroidery hoops or any other ring that will fit around your wrist.

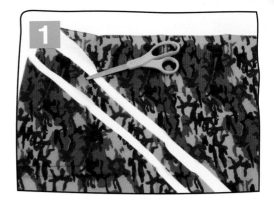

TRULY TERRIFIC TAPESTRY

Fashion a fun and funky tapestry out of fabric scraps.
Hang it on a wall to add pizazz to your favorite space!

What You Need:

scissors (both craft & fabric)

cardboard

ruler or measuring tape

fabric

hot glue gun

pom-poms or other
    decorations (optional)

What You Do:

1   Cut a piece of cardboard into your
    tapestry shape.

2   Cut strips of fabric about 2 inches
    (5 cm) wide and in varying lengths.

3   Arrange the strips in overlapping
    rows on the cardboard. The ends
    of the strips should hang off the
    edges. Glue the strips in place.

4   Turn the cardboard over and glue
    down the loose ends.

5   If you like, glue on pom-poms or
    other decorations!

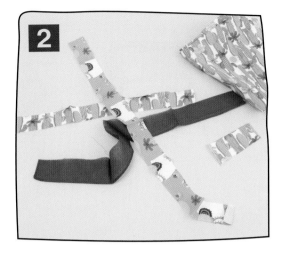

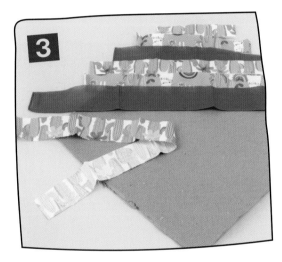

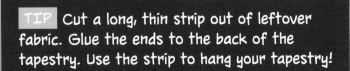

TIP Cut a long, thin strip out of leftover
fabric. Glue the ends to the back of the
tapestry. Use the strip to hang your tapestry!

21

"SOCK"-TOPUS
PIRATE

Aaargh! Imagine sailing around the world
with this sea creature buccaneer!

What You Need:

5 old socks
tennis ball
scissors (fabric)
mini rubber bands
hot glue gun
googly eyes
felt
scrap fabric

What You Do:

1 Put the tennis ball inside a sock. Layer another sock over the first. Repeat until four socks cover the tennis ball.

2 Cut two slits in each sock, running from the end to the base of the tennis ball. This will create eight strips of fabric, or octopus arms.

3 Knot each strip at the base of the tennis ball.

4 Twist a mini rubber band around the end of each arm.

5 Cut the toe off the last sock. Glue it to the octopus's head as a hat.

6 Decorate your pirate octopus! Glue on felt, googly eyes, and fabric scraps.

T-SHIRT TOTE

Turn an old T-shirt into a handy tote to carry
all your everyday essentials.

What You Need:

old T-shirt
scissors (fabric)
ruler or measuring tape

What You Do:

1 Turn the shirt inside out. Cut off the sleeves. Cut the neck to make it a bit wider.

2 Cut vertical strips through both layers of the shirt's bottom edge. Make each strip about 1 to 2 inches (2.5 to 5 cm) wide and about 3 inches (8 cm) long.

3 Tie each front strip to its matching back strip to close up the edge.

4 Turn the shirt right side out and fill your tote with your favorite things!

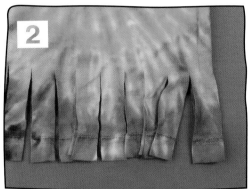

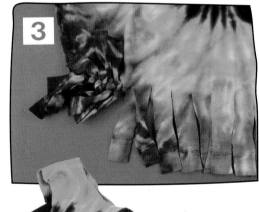

MONSTER FINGER PALS

Got one old winter glove lying around?
Give it a new life by transforming it
into spooky puppets for your fingers!

What You Need:

old winter glove

scissors (both craft & fabric)

craft foam

hot glue gun

googly eyes

decorative materials

What You Do:

1 Cut the fingers off the glove.

2 Cut teeth, wings, and other monster features out of the craft foam.

3 Glue googly eyes and the cut foam pieces to the fingers. Add other decorative materials to give your monsters flair. Be creative and use your imagination!

TIP Old rings, string, and chenille stems all make great decorative materials!

DOG'S BEST FRIEND

Make a brand-new dog toy out of an old pair of jeans.
Give it to your furry friend or to a dog shelter.

What You Need:

old pair of jeans or other denim fabric

scissors (fabric)

ruler or measuring tape

fabric scraps

tape

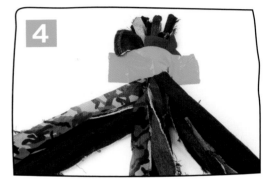

What You Do:

1 Cut the denim fabric into nine strips. Make each strip about 2 inches (5 cm) wide and 18 inches (46 cm) long.

2 Cut two more strips out of other fabric scraps. Make them each about 1 inch (2.5 cm) wide and 6 inches (15 cm) long.

3 Gather the ends of the long strips together. Wrap one short fabric strip around one end and tie it in place.

4 Tape the tied end to a table or other surface. Divide the long strips into three sections of three. Braid the sections together.

5 Tie the second short strip around the end of the braid to secure it.

TIP Add a pop of color to your dog toy by braiding in a contrasting color of fabric.

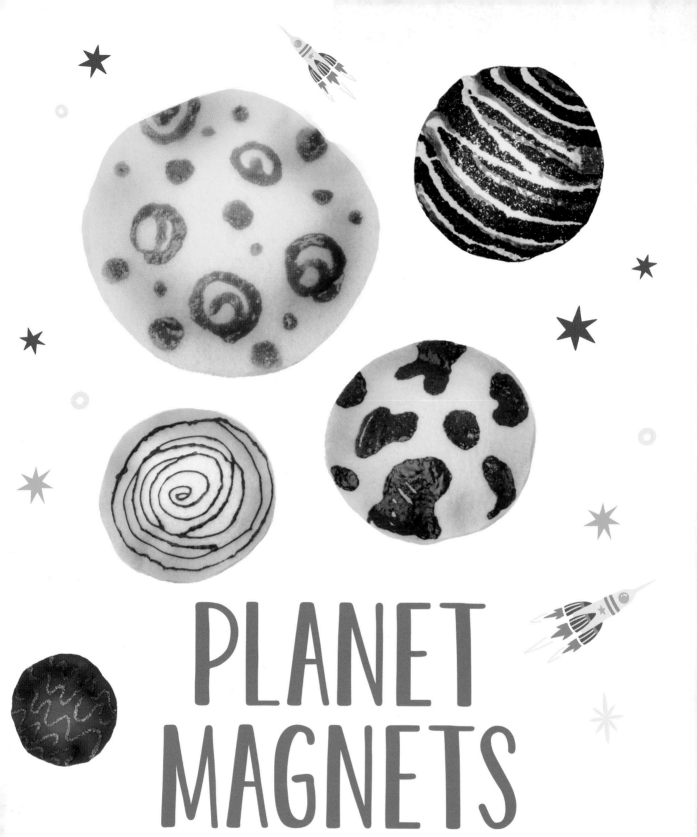

PLANET MAGNETS

These celestial 3D magnets will add out-of-this-world appeal to your locker or refrigerator.

What You Need:

felt

jar

marker

scissors
(fabric)

hot glue gun

fiberfill
stuffing

magnet

puffy fabric
paint

What You Do:

1 Trace the jar opening two times on the felt. Cut out the circles.

2 Put a line of glue around the edge of one circle, leaving a gap about 1 inch (2.5 cm) wide. Place the second circle on top of the first to glue them together.

3 Push stuffing through the opening until the circle is plump and full. Seal the opening with glue.

4 Glue a magnet to the back of the planet.

5 Decorate the planet with puffy fabric paint. Add land masses, swirls, and more!

Read More

Editors of Klutz. *Klutz: Sew Mini Animals*. New York: Scholastic, 2020.

Kenney, Karen Latchana. *No-Sew Pillows, Blankets, Fabric Crafts, and Other Bedroom Makeover Projects.* North Mankato, MN: Capstone Press, 2019.

Kuskowski, Alex. *Cool Refashioned Sweaters: Fun & Easy Fashion Projects.* Minneapolis: Abdo Publishing, 2016.

Internet Sites

Care.com: Easy No-Sew Kids' Crafts Ideas
care.com/c/stories/3914/easy-no-sew-kids-craft-ideas/

Dabbles and Babbles: 15 Fun and Easy Sewing Projects for Kids
dabblesandbabbles.com/15-fun-and-easy-sewing-projects-for-kids/

Play Ideas: 25 No-Sew Crafts for Kids
playideas.com/25-no-sew-cloth-activities/